REIKI

THE INSTRUCTORS' MANUALS

Norman W. Wilson, Ph.D.

Norman W. Wilson Ph.D.

REIKI

THE INSTRUCTORS' MANUALS

Published by

2018

ISBN: 978-1-78695-200-4

Cover by
SR Walker Designs

www.srwalkerdesigns.com

DEDICATION

To those who have no choice but to help others heal themselves.

ACKNOWLEDGMENTS

A very large thank you to many of my teachers: Angie Webster, Peggy Jentoft, Sonnet Godfrey, Owen Coleman, Lee Holden, Marie Diamond, Ashley Levy, Hank Manson, Tristan Truscott, Susanna Mantis, and Kain Ramsy. All have contributed to my endless search for ways to help others help themselves. For that, I am grateful.

Reiki Master, Norman W. WilsoOn, Ph.D.

FIRST MANUAL

LEVEL ONE

ATTUNEMENT ONE

FIRST MANUAL

LEVEL ONE

ATTUNEMENT ONE

CHAPTER ONE

INTRODUCTION:

Reiki (pronounced ray-kee) is a natural healing system based upon the flow of universal energy. Rei means universal and ki means life force. The concept is as old as is humanity. It is a laying-on-of hands technique somewhat modified from its earlier religious usage. My first experience with the latter approach was back in the early 1940's. A young girl was very ill and all medical attempts to help her failed. The local priest called for a Healing. He asked that those who were pure of heart in their desire to help this little girl come to the church, join hands in a long line. The first person in that line held his hand out to the priest, who in turn placed his hand on the little girl's head. She got well. People called it a wonder, a metaphysical experience in today's terms.

In our modern world, we understand the transfer and redirection of energy. Solar panels absorb the light of the sun and convert it into electricity.

Reiki is based on several healing modalities grounded in Asia, especially Chinese and Japanese medicines. Fast forward to the 20th Century, specifically, the 1920's. It was during this time period that the use of energy to help to heal was, you might say, rediscovered. Dr. Mikao Usui a Japanese doctor came to this approach after spending time in a Zen monastery. Taking what he understood, he applied it to his practice and began to train others. Two others have had a significant influence on its development and recognition: Dr. Cjikorp Hayashi and Mrs. Hawayo Takata.

Dr. Hayashi opened a healing clinic in Tokyo and is responsible for developing a set of complex hand positions to be used during a healing session. Hawayo Takata is given credit for bringing Reiki to Hawaii, and then to mainland United States, to Canada and finally to Europe. As is all too often the case, when one enjoys success with a partner, there is a split. In 1980 two splintered groups were formed, the Reiki Alliance and the American International Reiki Association, Inc.

Divergent View: I want to stop here for a moment and express a couple of my own opinions. In much of the literature surrounding Reiki the following term is used; Reiki Universal Energy. If my understanding is correct Reiki really means universal energy (Life force). So why say Energy, Energy when talking about Reiki? Why not simply say Reiki or Universal Energy?

Second, I want to address, early on, the issue of hands-on treatment. I do not recommend physically touching a client unless there is a written statement you, as a healer, may do so. And then, I strongly urge stating which body parts may be touched: shoulders, back of neck, front, back and top of head, and feet. I suggest hovering hands over chest and abdomen. Some Reiki practitioners do not physically touch a client's body and others do. It a caution for today's world of sexual harassment.

Third, I do not recommend clients remove their clothing. I do ask them to remove their shoes and socks before getting on the treatment table. I use essential oils in my Reiki treatment and I begin with the feet. More about feet later.

<u>Some Concerns:</u> Often beginning Reiki practitioners worry about what treating others does to them. Giving Reiki does not diminish your energy. You, as a Reiki Practitioner, do not generate the energy. It flows through you, much as does an electrical current flow through a wire. You are a CONDUIT.

As a Reiki Practitioner, you have to be aware of the potential of picking up negative energy from a client. Such energy exudes throughout the treatment room and may linger. Cleans the room after use, wash your own hands, give yourself a spritz of lavender hydrosol, and change the massage table covering. If you use a light blanket to cover the client, change that as you receive a new client.

Payment and what to charge may be an issue for some. Traditional Reiki says charge otherwise your gift will not be really appreciated; thus, the result may not be as hoped for. This does not mean you can't gift someone.

Sometimes, as a Reiki Practitioner, you may have a client who is in need of spiritual healing. Reiki can help. However, if the issue is emotional you need to anticipate crying, other emotional outbursts, or a rejection. A nearby box of tissues is always a good idea. Soft music playing in the background is generally accepted.

During your healing session do not carry on a running conversation. Check to see if the client is comfortable.

HOW REIKI WORKS:

Most of the literature refers to Reiki as "life force" or "Universal Life Force Energy." For me, such statements do not tell me very much. I prefer using vibration or universal vibration. My reason for this is simple: Everything vibrates. Vibration creates energy. Humans, plants, animals, rocks, water, air, dirt all vibrate. Some Reiki Practitioners believe energy flows through their hands but is not generated by them. For me, that flies in the face of scientific evidence that all things vibrate. You vibrate and as a healer, you use your natural vibration to merge with the vibrations of the universe and then redirect the flow of energy to where it is needed in a client's body. Think in terms of a tuning fork. Once it is struck, it vibrates at a certain speed or hertz. You feel that vibration. Different tuning forks have different vibrational frequencies. You change your vibrational frequencies as directed by those of your client's body. And therein lies a secret to Reiki Healing's success.

It is suggested by some researchers that perhaps Reiki's physical, mental, emotional, and its spiritual healing effect is actually triggered on a sub-physical level. This level has been called the biofield.

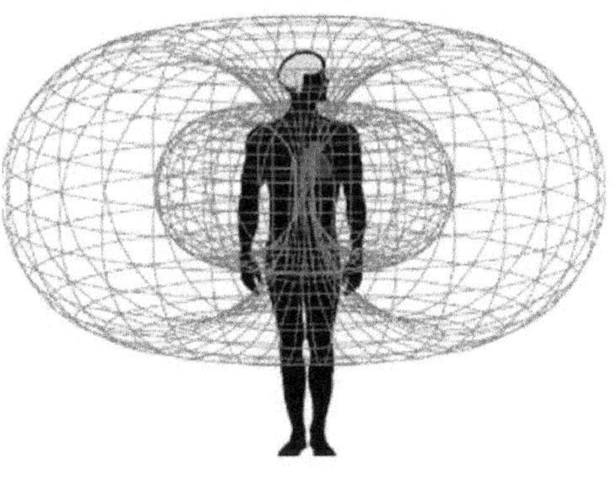

The Biofield: In 1994 a group of scientists associated with the National Institute of Health coined the word *biofield* to describe the energy and information that surrounds and interpenetrates one's body. This biofield contains electromagnetic energy which is measurable. It also contains something called subtle energy or chi. With a little training and practice, one can learn to actually see this field. It's commonly called an *Aura.* Since all things are vibrational energy, I believe we can see the auras of plants, animals, and non-living matter such as crystals. Another name for biofield and is sometimes used interchangeably is bioplasma. An excellent discourse on the biofield is Eileen McKusick's book titled ***Tuning the Human Biofield: Healing with Vibrations Sound Therapy.***

WHAT REIKI DOES:

The most obvious thing Reiki does is to help a person heal her or himself. It can, and *can* is the operative word here, bring relief to the suffering. In many instances, it can alleviate that suffering. Suffering is a large all-inclusive word. It includes the physical, emotional, mental, and or spiritual realms of the human being. As an aside, it works with animals and plants.

There is an inherent danger of misunderstanding here. There is no guarantee that Reiki will relieve anything. I strongly suggest that you never promise relief or a cure. It is good practice to tell your client he or she may or may not feel anything during a treatment session or afterwards. I generally suggest a three day window and that what the client may feel will be subtle.

Reiki treatment is now being offered in some hospitals in conjunction with a person's medical treatment. Always check with the client about their medical treatment, prescriptions, and previous forms of supportive treatment. A good professional habit is to suggest the client keep his or her medical doctor in the loop.

One of the inherent principles of Reiki is that it does no harm and cannot be used to bring harm to any life form. The Practitioner can do harm by not being honest with a client, by making false promises, or by undercutting contemporary standard medical treatment.

I want to come back to two words in the first paragraph of this section: emotional and mental. They are not the same nor do they reference the same processes. Emotional refers to feelings: Hurt feelings caused by rejection, trauma, the death of a loved one, or a perceived offense. Mental refers to those processes in the brain that relate to cognition and regulation of bodily functions.

Reiki will help one's natural spiritual flow if it has been compromised. Spirituality, as used here, does not have a religious connotation. Further, Reiki has no religious base or affiliation. It will not produce enlightenment. It will help tone the whole person in preparation for significant meditation practices.

Reiki helps the body's natural ability to heal itself. It increases one's vitality and stamina. It involves the whole person. It releases blocked energy, promotes relaxation and stress reduction.

WHAT REIKI IS NOT:

Reiki is not a cult. It is not a religion even though it is reported Dr. Mikao Usui came to this after being in a meditative state, and extensive fasting. There is no dogma but there are set procedures. Like many things over time, these procedures have been modified or changed. This does not diminish the value of Reiki.

> Reiki is a complementary medicine practice that uses putative energy fields to affect health.
>
> The National Center for Complementary and Integrative Health.

LEVEL ONE

CHAPTER TWO

ATTUNEMENT

Bear with me while I bring a tad more science to the Reiki table. It does seem that everyone these days references Quantum Physics to support their supposition(s). It's value for Reiki lies in QP's proof that the fundamental building block of all existence is energy. Further, that energy is created by vibration. Reiki uses that vibrating energy to direct and or change the flow of a client's energy pattern. This is huge! There are 37.2 trillion cells in the human body. That equates to 7 billion billion billion atoms. That's 7 followed by 27 zeros. You should view this a wonderful menu to work with rather than trying to move the impossible.

Attunement, like healing, relies upon the molecular structure of your body. Attunement is more than healing you, it is creating a healer. To that end, you will experience a short cleansing. Usually, this involves the whole room and the use of an incense. Lavender, white sage, rosemary, and Palo Santo are commonly used. Some Reiki professionals recommend a 21 day cleansing both physical and spiritual. For me, that is not at all necessary.

Then the Five Principles of Reiki are recited. The purpose of this recitation is to set the stage for the primary intention (more will be said about intention later) but for now, it is simply what you want.

THE FIVE PRINCIPLES OF REIKI

1. For today, I will be grateful.
2. For today, I will not be angry.
3. For today I will not worry.
4. For today, I will work honestly.
5. For today, I will respect all life.

What is my reason for using the phrase "For today"? Why not simply say the intent. Basically, the reason is to remind you to be in the present moment.

Reiki is passed from the master to the student through what is called an attunement. This passing of energy allows the student to connect to the energy of the universe. What is really involved in an attunement? In Level One, you are instructed in the use of three very specific Reiki symbols; each representing a different characteristic of Reiki energy. These three characteristics are:

1. Power
2. mental/emotional balance
3. distance healing.

Learn each of these symbols. Draw them physically several times. Next, draw them in the air with your hand. Then close your eyes and draw them within your mind.

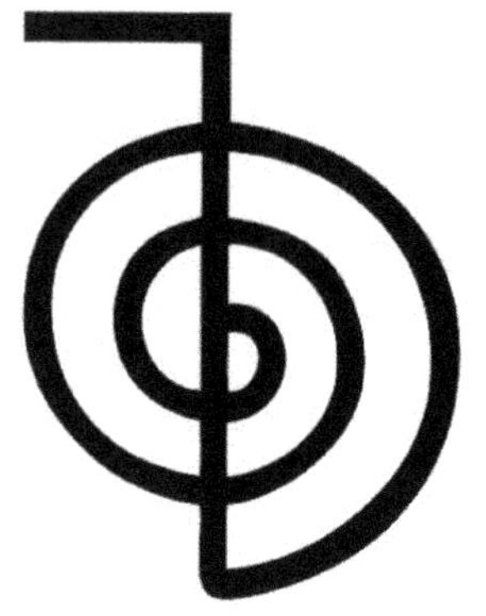

The first symbol is the power symbol. Its name is Cho-ko-rei. (pronounced as Koo Ko Ray) It literally means *place all the powers* of *the universe here*. It functions as a switch does on a lamp. When the switch is pushed the lamp immediately sheds light. Cho-ko-rei immediately increases the practitioner's ability to channel energies. Please note the word *energies* is plural.

SEI HE KI

The second symbol is called Sei He-Ki. (pronounced as Say Hi Key) Traditionally it is said to mean God and Man become one. It brings together the brain and the body. It works to focus and harmonize the subconscious with the physical body. It promotes a zeroing in on a client.

The third symbol used in Level One is for distance healing. It is Hon She Ze Sho Nen. (pronounced as Hon-ShaZee-Show-Nen)And is most likely the one you will use often during your first healing work. It's a good one to practice with on your pets if they are in another room or a family member. Once you have gained some confidence try it with someone on another street, or in a neighboring town. Eventually, you will be tuned to do it world wide. It literally means "no past, no present, no future."

Some, however, say it means "The Buddha in me contacts the Buddha in you."

Most authorities in Reiki point out there is a correct way to draw the Hon She Ze Sho Nen symbol. It is illustrated on the following page.

DRAWING HON SHA ZE SHO NEN:

Pinterest #137

Follow the numbers. Note that this particular image has an extra line at the bottom, line 20. It is not necessary.

DISTANCE HEALING:

Distance healing is just that, healing at a distance from you. Because Reiki is so powerful, it allows you to expand your healing abilities well beyond where you are physically located. In fact, it expands your healing reach beyond the so-called limitations of time and space. You can send spiritual energy beyond your physical touch of a client. In some Reiki circles, this is referred to as "Absentee Healing."

The rationale behind using Absentee Healing instead of Distant Healing is interesting and may provide further study for the Practitioner. The AHT (Absentee Healing Technique) claims it comes from a state of Oneness. By that, it is meant that you and Reiki are connected to everything. Diona Ceniza a Level III Reiki Practitioner states . . . "you aren't "sending" Reiki, instead you're feeling *one* with another person and sharing Reiki in that way."[1] Ceniza further claims that distance suggests a separation which just the opposite of being in a state of Oneness.

During the distance healing, you should add a mantra. A good example of Reiki mantra you can use is *Om Mani Padme Hum* (pronounced as ohm mah nee pahd may hum). Enjoying worldwide popularity, this mantra produces a compassionate state. This mantra says that if the mind and the heart become one, nothing is impossible. It exudes the compassion energy found in the Usui emotional and mental symbol of Hon Sha Ze Sho Nen. Om Mani Padme Hum mantra invokes powerful benevolent attention and blessing; the embodiment of compassion.

---

[1] From Distance Reiki: The Beginner's Guide to Distance Healing. Center for True Health. New York, NY. 2014

HOW TO DO DISTANCE HEALING:

I was taught you had to have a person's permission before you could send them Reiki. Current literature is challenging that. If you are asked to send Reiki to someone's friend or relative do it even if that friend or relative has not personally requested you do so. Here are the steps:

1. Do a cleanse of yourself, meditate for at least fifteen minutes. Burn some incense. Place a few power crystals around you. Softly say this mantra: "Om Mani Padme Hum" [2]

2. If you have a photo of the person look at that. Concentrate on the photo.

3. Draw the symbol for Hon Sha Ze Sho Nen.

4. Say Hon Sha Ze Sho Nen three times.

---

[2] The word *Mani* means "jewel" or "bead", *Padme* is the "lotus flower" (the Buddhist sacred flower), and *Hum* represents the spirit of enlightenment. It is commonly carved onto rocks, known as *mani* stones, or else it is written on paper which is inserted into prayer wheels.

5 Rub your hands together. As you do so, say aloud or to yourself, "Universal energy go to (person's name and if you know where she or he is located, say that.) For example:" Universal energy go to Betty in London and in your infinite wisdom help her heal herself." Some practitioners add "for the highest good."

6. Cup your hands together, leaving a space for you to blow into.

7. Blow in the space your cupped hands.

8. Open your hands, and shove them out and upward. Use some force.

USING A DOLL IN DISTANCE HEALING:

If a photo of the person to whom you are sending distance healing is not available you may use a doll or a toy stuffed animal. Using the doll as a replica of the client, perform the healing ritual as you would if the person was physically with you. The sole purpose for using a doll or stuffed animal is to help you concentrate. A general rule of thumb is to have a set time for your recipient to receive the healing.

A number of years ago I worked with a young man who had MS and was wheelchair bound. A distance of 2,000 miles separated us. It was agreed that Josh would be up at 9:00 AM. I asked that he be at a table and have the following items on his table: a lit candle, white sage burning, two clear quartz crystals, one held in each hand, and to have placed two drops of Thieves Oil on each wrist. I also asked him to have placed two drops of Frankincense in the center of his forehead. (Third Eye Chakra.) The healing was done every day for a month. Josh did this in addition to contemporary medical treatment. Today, he is out of the wheel chair and walking. He uses a cane. Can I claim that my distance healing made this happen? I would be totally remiss to say it did but I can say it did no harm, and that it was one more tool in the arsenal he uses to fight his disease.

Below is a photo of the cloth doll I used in my sessions with Josh. It was made by a friend.

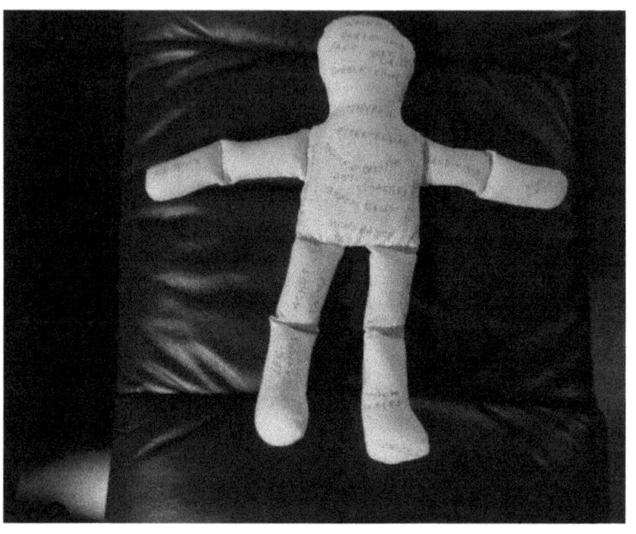

Photo by Suzanne V. Wilson

One of the issues you may face is charging for your services. Some Reiki Practitioners have a set fee for distance healing. They also establish a specific amount of time as well as the date and how often the session will take place. Others do not charge for distance healing. For example, one may charge five dollars per minute, minimum charge being $25.

CREATING AND USING A REIKI BOX FOR DISTANCE HEALING

Another approach to sending Reiki over distance is to create Reiki Box. This is especially useful if you want to send Reiki to several people at once. The box should be small enough to comfortably hold in your hands. You can use any box, make one of your own, or buy one. You may decorate your box or not.

Steps for Using A Reiki Box

1. On a sheet of paper, write the name of your client, any identifying information such as the nature of illness, or issue, location, general age, adult, child, youth, baby. An example: Bob, lung cancer, Denver, mid-thirties, non-smoker. Had chemo and radiation. If a photo is available attach that to the paper.

2. Using a colored marker, draw the Reiki Distance Symbol (Hon Sha Sho Ze Nen) directly onto the paper. Fold the paper and photo and place it in the box. Do this for each of your distance clients.

3. Close the box.

4. Draw the Reiki Distance Symbol on the palm of each hand.

5. Hold the box in both hands, point toward the sky, and say, "Reiki go to these people and in your infinite wisdom do all you can to help them heal themselves."

6. Pause for a moment in thanks and then wash your hands. Always wash your hands before and after a healing session.

Reiki Healing Box

Photo by Suzanne V. Wilson

PREPARING FOR YOUR ATTUNEMENT:

Depending on your background and own choices, you may choose to reconnect with your own spiritual practice before your attunement begins. This may be sitting still and meditating or it may be going into a yoga pose, doing some stretching exercises.

It is often recommended that you avoid alcohol, caffeine, sugar, pot and eating heavy foods the day before your attunement. Limit television viewing and repeat the five principles of Reiki (page 10) many times during the day before the scheduled attunement.

WHAT SHOULD YOU EXPECT?

For some, having a reiki attunement is a powerful spiritual experience. Others feel a surge in energy, either warm or cool. You may feel a slight shudder or a tingling throughout your body. You may sense an increase I n your intuitive awareness and psychic sensitivity. You may feel you can 'read' people more clearly. Or, you may actually feel nothing different. A few days later you may experience a spurt of energy or creativity. After doing your first healing, you may feel lightened. No two people who have the same exact experience.

The Attunement Ceremony:

Initiation is often used to name the First Attunement one receives as part of their Reiki training. **Attunement** was the early term adopted by practitioners of energy medicine. It was originally developed by Lloyd Arthur Meeker (d. 1954). Meeker taught and practiced **Attunement** as a central feature of his spiritual teaching and ministry, Emissaries of Divine Light. Today, attunement describes how reactive a person is to another's emotional, mental and physical needs. A person who is well attuned will respond with appropriate healing behaviors based on another person's state. The ceremony is designed to help the future Reiki practitioner to tune in to a client's needs. It is that finesse that directs the healing session.

Each Reiki Master, especially those who have attained Third Level and or additional certifications, will create her or his own ceremonial procedures. Some are as simple as the laying of the Master's hands on the head of the inductee. Incense, soft music, lowered lights, crystals, and essential oils may be used as part of the ceremony.

The bottom line for the initiate is the acceptance of the transfer of energy from the Master. After that, the individual can then practice Reiki on her or himself, and do distance healing. So how long should you practice before taking your second attunement? Dr. Beena Rani Goel[3] suggests 21 days. This assumes that everyone has the same level of skills. As an educator with over 40 years of experience, I know that not everyone learns at the same speed. It is safe to say you should, at the very least, practice every day until one day before your next attunement. I like to have a week before each attunement.

To enable this immediate practice there are certain hand positions that need to be mastered. Remember, it is one's hands that transfer the healing energy. Practice these hand positions until they are a second nature to you. There is some mild dispute about what part of the body you should begin your self-treatment or your distant healing. Logic suggests you should first heal yourself before attempting to heal someone else. With that said, where do you begin your self-healing? Some practitioners believe you should begin with your head and work your way down

---

[3] Author of Healing Through Reiki. Health Care Trust. Belgaum, India. 2011.

during your self-healing. This is also true if you are working with a client. Others suggest you begin with the client's feet and work your way up to the head. When I am working with a client in a healing session I tend to begin with the feet, the point of all grounding. Bottom line is, it's your choice.

The Initiation Steps for Attunement One, Level One:

The client is in a seated position, yoga style, on a mat or seated in a chair with both feet flat on the floor and hands held in the prayer position a few inches from the heart chakra. The client's eyes should be closed. I prefer a chair. I also have some soft music playing in the background. Some of the **Solfeggio** frequencies, especially the 528H works nicely as do Native American Flute or Jonathan Goldman's The Divine Name: I AM.

1. Place your non-dominate hand on the client's head. (Crown Chakra) With your dominate hand draw Hon-Sha Ze Sho Nen,

then draw Sei He Ki on the client's left shoulder and finally moving in a clock-wise direction, draw Cho Ku Rei on the client's right shoulder.

2. Come to the front of the client, cup her or his hands, still in prayer position, in yours also in prayer position. Make sure your thumbs lap over the client's hands. Gently move the hands from your Heart Chakra to the client's Heart Chakra. Do this three times.

3. Place the client's left hand her or his right chest. Open her or his right hand and with your index finger draw the Hon Sha Ze Sho Nen symbol on the person's palm. Do this three times.

4. Now take the client's right hand and place it on her or his left chest. Open the left hand and draw the symbol for Cho Ku Rei. Do this three times.

5. Smudge the client with Palo Santo, white sage and copal.

6. Offer herbal tea or lemon infused water.

Basically, this ends the first attunement. Other Reiki Masters may add other items. If they do, it does not diminish the initiation. Each teacher makes the system her or his own.

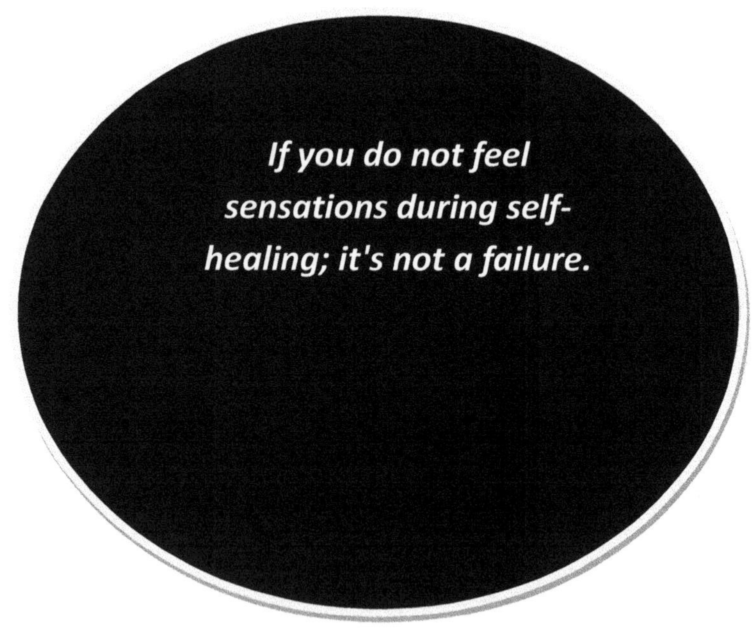

NOTES

THE REIKI HAND POSITIONS FOR SELF-HEALING[4]

[4] From Pinterest.

ATTUNEMENT SESSION FOLLOW-UP

After the attunement, there is a follow-up. Students are asked to go into meditation or relaxing yoga pose. This should be about 10 to 15 minutes in length. After which the client and instructor exchange feelings, thoughts, questions about what had transpired during the attunement. This is like a debriefing session.

It is not a matter of faith; it is a matter

of practice.

Thich Nhat Hanh

ENERGY EXERCISES

As a healer, energy becomes all important to you and in what you do for your clients. The following exercises are designed to help you with your energy.

Exercise 1.

This exercise is designed to help you tune into your own energy grid or energy body. Simple, yet effective, I strongly urge you to practice any one of these on a daily basis until noticing your energy is really second nature to you.

1. Sit or lie down, making sure you are comfortable. A key here is to let your body completely relax.

2. Use pillows, light weight blanket. If you chose to use a traditional yoga position be sure your body is well supported.

3. Place one hand on your abdomen and the other on your heart chakra. Slowly tune

into your breathing; note the easy natural rhythm of your hands as they rise and fall.

Notice how your body temperature feels. Do you feel energy swirling around you? It can be very subtle.

Exercise 2.

This exercise is to help bring about a focused energy balancing. Energy can be directed to specific body parts, chakras, or meridians.

1. Get comfortable. Do three sets of breaths through your nose, exhaling through your slightly open mouth.

2. Use the first two fingers of your dominate hand and gently place them on a chakra, or meridian. Don't hurry this. Gradually, you should feel the movement of energy.

Exercise 3. I call this the Haaaah Exercise. Traditionally it is called Ujjayi (pronounced oo-jai). In some of the literature about breathing, it is called "Ocean Breath." Besides being a balancing influence on the entire cardiorespiratory system, Ujjayi releases stress increases the flow of oxygen to your blood and thus boosting your energy. It helps clear the brain and body of toxins. I come back to this in Level Two Attunement.

1. Close your mouth and start to breathe through your nose.to breath in and out through your nose.

2. Make sure your inhalation through your nose is deeper than your normal breathing. By deeper, it is meant you should draw air in for a longer period of time.

3. Place your tongue behind your upper teeth, open your mouth and exhale.

4. Do this six times.

Energy Depletion Photo by Suzanne V. Wilson

SECOND MANUAL

LEVEL TWO

ATTUNEMENT TWO

SECOND MANUAL

CHAPTER ONE

LEVEL TWO

ATTUNEMENT TWO

INTRODUCTION:

Reiki Level One focused on connectivity, foundations for the hands-on -experience in the use of Reiki, practice with distance healing. With the completion of Level One, you were certified to heal yourself and do distance healing. Level Two and its subsequent attunement emphasizes the mental and emotional aspect of Reiki healing.

At this level, you are moved beyond the traditional to perhaps a more esoteric conceptual approach which takes you into the enlightened circle of the professionals.

You are reminded to continue your practicing of what you learned in Level One. The old sawing of "Practice Makes Perfect" holds true.

Training at Level Two is based on Dr. Mikao Usui's Three Pillars of Reiki. Additional Reiki symbols, their meaning, and use will be introduced. The Three Pillars of Reiki are Gassho, Reiji-Ho, and Chiryo.

Gassho: (Pronounced gas-ho or gash-sho). Gassho means bring the hands together in prayer pose and represents the union of the divine within yourself. It also involves bowing to the person you meet. The bowing is formalized and should never be executed haphazardly. Hold your shoulders straight; do not bend them forward. The palm of your hands should be facing one another, be about three inches from our chest.

Bow from the waste, keeping the head aligned with the floor. Bow slowly and return to the standing position slowly. The bow will help establish a professional bond between you and your clients.

Gassho meditation should be used at the beginning of each Reiki healing session. Actually, it should be a part of your daily routine, a part of your lifestyle. It is recommended the meditation should be 15 to 30 minutes each morning and each evening before retiring. This, I believe, is an unreasonable demand for the modern world with all its time demands. Another stress just because you forgot to do the meditation is not needed. Five minutes will work as well as 30 minutes. The goal, if you want to call it that, is to experience and relish the stillness within and become fully present in your body. It's an opportunity to connect with your higher self.

In the event, you are not familiar with mediating follow these simple steps.

1. Sit in a quiet place where you will not be disturbed. Sit in a comfortable chair, on a meditation cushion or on a yoga mat.

2. The room should be dimly lit. Play some soft, quite music.

3. Make sure your spine is straight, close your eyes, bring your hands together in Gassho position. (prayer positon). There is no need to apply pressure to your hands.

4. You can set a timer or use your intuition.

5. Bring your attention to your body: head, chest, arms, abdomen, legs, and feet.

6. As you end your meditation slowly open your eyes to slits and gradually open them all the way. Be careful when you stand. Give yourself a couple of minutes to adjust to the upright position.

Reiji-Ho

Like the word Reiki, Reiji-Ho is a two part word with each part having a meaning. In this case, Reiji means "indication of Reiki power" and Ho means "methods." Dr. Usui has recommended three specific rituals for Practitioners to do before each client treatment. These have been somewhat modified to meet current needs and I added one, thus creating four rituals.

1. After washing your hands, fold them in prayer fashion in front of your chest. Use the Gassho posture and close your eyes. At this point, you are to connect to your Reiki power by asking that it flow through you.

2. You should, within a very few minutes, feel a change. Acknowledge it. You may notice it in your crown chakra, in your heart or in your hands. Here is where you may use the distance symbol. It will help connect you to Reiki power. Draw the symbol in your mind and repeat its name three times. Do this in your mind or very softly aloud.

3. Set your intention for your client. Be very specific.

4. Hold your folded hands in front of your Third Eye and ask Reiki to guide your hands to where the energy is needed in your client.

As a point of interest, as a future Reiki Practitioner, learn to trust your hands during a healing session with a client. They serve as your intuitive antenna. If you sense you should move, let your hands indicate where you should move them.

Chiryo:

The third Pillar is called Chiryo (pronounced like cheerio). It simply means *treatment*. While the client is on the massage table, hold your dominant hand above the client's crown chakra and wait until there is an impulse or rather an inclination or inspiration that the hand should move. Let it! During the treatment, give your hands free rein. They will take you where the client's needs are. They hands will remain where there is an issue until it is resolved; that is, the client is experiencing pain in a shoulder for example, and the pain lessens or goes away.

Reiki and the Sacred Symbols:

In Level Two, Reiki sacred symbols take on an even more important role. Think of them as keys to the energy vault. Perhaps thinking of these symbols as portals to universal energy will be helpful. As the course work progresses you will learn you can activate the power of the symbols in a variety of ways. You have met one in Level One, drawing the symbol on paper, in the air, and in your mind. Others include chanting and intending. Of these, the intention is by far the most important. And this brings me to one of my favorite talking points—intentions and their significance.

> There is always a gap between intention and action. Paulo Coelho

In my book, *How to Get What You REALLY Want*[5] I devote most of the book to the issue and question of intention. The first chapter explains what an intention is. It is short and I include some of it here.

Brenna Yovanoff in *The Replacement* writes "Intention is one of the most powerful forces there is. What you mean when you do a thing will always determine the outcome. This law creates the world." The most powerful force there is? What a pronouncement that is!

An intention is a state of mind in which there is a commitment, a fulfilling of a particular action, or desire. [In Reiki it is both action and desire] Furthermore, intention involves mental action or planning. This is simply another way of saying commitment. According to WORD, commitment means binding yourself intellectually and physically to a course of action. Three words, commitment, action, and binding must be married.

Fundamentally, intention is a function and as such, it is one that is designed to accomplish a very specific task. All too often, we make our intention too generalized in stating what is that we want, desire, or need.

---

[5] Wilson, Norman W. PhD. Surry, England. Zadkiel Publishing Paperback. 2018. p. 9

Even today, there is some disagreement over these "sacred" symbols being written down even during a training class, being made visible to clients, and to the public. The Internet has made them no longer sacrosanct. As it is true with the forward movement of a system, subtle changes take place. The symbols you will learn and use during this course are most likely modifications of those originally used by Dr. Usui. Even as you practice drawing them, your strokes may not be at the same angle, width, or intensity as those I show you. It's no big deal. The intention behind those symbols is!

Be aware of the fact that none of the Reiki symbols can be used to bring harm to another living entity. A short divergence. A person that I know was in a negative relationship with her spouse. It wasn't physical but emotional abuse. Over coffee one day someone there remembered I used a doll in my distance healing and suggested I bring it next time. I did. Immediately one person said, "Great. Stick a pin in the heart and maybe it will kill her husband." Laughter. I gently admonished the group and went on to offer to do a healing for the heart chakra for the man in question.

By the way, the symbols themselves hold no power and have no effect unless the user has been attuned. If you happen to leave a copy of the symbols laying around don’t' worry.

For now, I want to revisit two of the power symbols introduced in the First Level: The power symbols of Cho Ku Rei and Sei He Ki.

Note that the central anchor of Cho Ku Rei starts at the left in Figure A and on the right in Figure B. There is the difference in the thickness of the pen strokes as well as white space between the lines. This does not impact the power of the symbols. Now, look at Figures C and D.

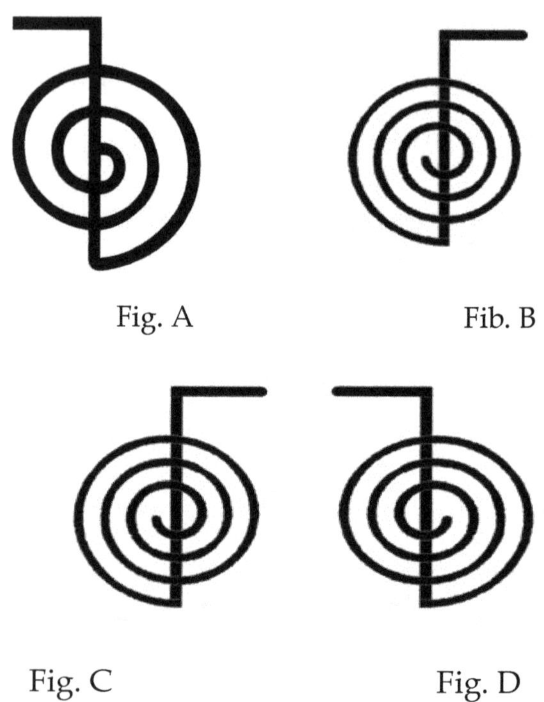

Fig. A

Fib. B

Fig. C

Fig. D

A portal is created that allows the full flow of energy. Place this in a discrete place in your office.

With just a little imagination one can see that this could be an outline of a human skull showing a configuration of the brain. Two chakras come into play during the use of the Reiki symbols: First is the crown chakra which houses the brain, a center of energy power; second, is the heart chakra, the second most powerful energy source in the human body. Both the brain and heart are also centers for emotions.

FIG. E

Creating a Cho Ku Rei Protective Shield:

Protecting yourself, or shielding as it is often called is an important part of the healing processes. As a healer, you are generally more susceptible to various energies, some of which may be negative. At some point in your life, you have walked into a room and felt an unease about it. Perhaps you have been some place and felt a sudden change in energy. A recent experience reminded me that I should write about protecting yourself.

Half-way through my yoga class, I felt a very large energy shift in the room. It was oppressive. It was an energy suck-up and by that I mean there was an energy drain in the class. I mentally did a protective shield. The oppressive feelings went away. I later spoke to my teacher and she too had felt a significant change in the room. Neither of us could account for the source causing this change. She immediately said she would white sage the whole area. What do you do if you are not in a position to white sage the area in which you are in?

Summitta A. Mazumdar [6] has suggested creating a Cho Ku Rei pyramid shield. She indicates you should draw the symbol for Cho Ku Rei three times; thus, creating a visual pyramid. You can physically do this by using your finger to draw the symbol in the air or imagine it in your mind's eye.

If you are going into a place with which you are not familiar with how do you protect yourself? I suggest using sea salt. Place a quarter of a teaspoon of sea salt in a small plastic bag and carry it with you. If that doesn't appeal to you, carry a piece of black tourmaline with you. If you are a woman, a piece of jewelry with black tourmaline works very nicely.

Finally, remember you are in control.

Grounding:

As a Reiki Practitioner, you should always be aware of being grounded. What does it mean

[6] Masumdar, Saummitta A. Cho Ku Rei Pyramid Shield. Reiki Rays.com, July 28, 2018.

to be grounded? Simply put, being grounded means to be very much present in the here and now. I like to say it is being very aware of your own energy field. I mean you are to have your energy field securely present, in your body, in present time, connected clearly to your present identity. It is to be the center of your focus. Such a focus forces into the background all the rattling and noise going on in your brain about past and or future events.

The old uncomplimentary word *scatterbrain* comes to mind. You race from one idea to another, from one thought to another without ever connecting any of the dots. It's a life filled with " I could-a and I should-a." When you stop the continual brain conference you are grounded.

There are misconceptions about being grounded. Some are quite outrageous. You become ungrounded by traveling in an airplane. Another one is being outside in the dirt and barefoot. How about hugging a tree for an hour? It is not a loss of environmental connectivity that causes the problem. Our disconnectedness from ourselves is the cause.

ACTIVITIES TO HELP YOU GET GROUNDED:

There are several activities designed to help you to become grounded. The first one deals with breathing and the use of a mantra. A mantra originally was a Hindu or Buddhist word or sound repeated to help in meditation. Today it may be a word, sound, or a phrase that is repeated. It does not have to be Hindu or Buddhist.

1. Breathing at a set rhythm and pace is an easy way to calm your mind. It can be done anywhere at any time. Taking deep breaths will almost instantly calm you. Breathe through your nose and allow the air to travel all the way down to your abdomen. Exhale audibly allowing the air to come up from the abdomen. Do this for five to ten minutes. As you breathe in, say this mantra or create one of your own: "I am calm." As you exhale say, "I am at peace."

2. Meditation requires you to be stationary and definitely not driving any vehicle. I do not believe one can totally empty his or her mind. (Monks who have been mediating for many hours a day for years might come close but for most people, this is not necessary. The game plan is to quiet the mind. I have an appreciation for Mindful Awareness. At its simplest level, Mindful Awareness means recognizing any thought that comes into your head and letting it go. It means not trying to shut your thoughts out.

During your meditation you should be in a comfortable position, seated or laying down. You may wish to use a mudra. A mudra is hand gesture used in Hindu and Buddhist ceremonies as well as in some yoga practices. The *Dhyana* mudra is recommended. To do the *Dhyana* mudra, simply sit with your hands facing upward, right hand resting on top of your left palm. The right hand, representing enlightenment and higher spiritual faculties, rests over the left hand, representing the world of maya, or illusion.

3, Soaking your feet in a salt water bath. In a pan large enough for your feet, add warm water, and one tablespoon full of sea salt. Soak your feet for ten to fifteen minutes. An added touch here is to put five to ten drops of rosemary essential oil into the water.

4. Connecting to the earth by taking a walk, sitting in your garden, watching the stars at night. Take time out to listen to the natural sounds around you: birds chirping, bees bussing. If you have flowers in your yard stop and look at them, notice their shapes and scents. Watch the clouds. When you were a child, did you look at the clouds and see animals and faces? Do that again.

5. Crystals are a wonderful way to get grounded, to get back in touch with yourself. Because, like you and everything else, they vibrate it's a good idea to select crystals that you feel good about. As with anything else,

follow your instincts when selecting which crystals you will use. I like and use clear quartz, amethyst, hematite and black tourmaline. Carry one or more crystals with you, place them around your computer, on your night stand.

6. Essential oils are an easy and pleasant way to get grounded. The inherent issue with essential oils is making sure of their purity. A 2018 report indicates that 60% of essential oils on the market are contaminated. Peppermint from India, Lavender from France and Tea Tree from Australia are said to be contaminated. The European Union recently banned 4,000 such oils because they were contaminated with talc. I do not recommend buying your essential oils from your local food outlet.

Lavender, Rosemary, Frankincense, Lemon and Ylang ylang are excellent.

BE GRATEFUL FOR THE BLESSINGS THAT ARE ON THE WAY

THREE REIKI SYMBOLS FOR LEVEL TWO

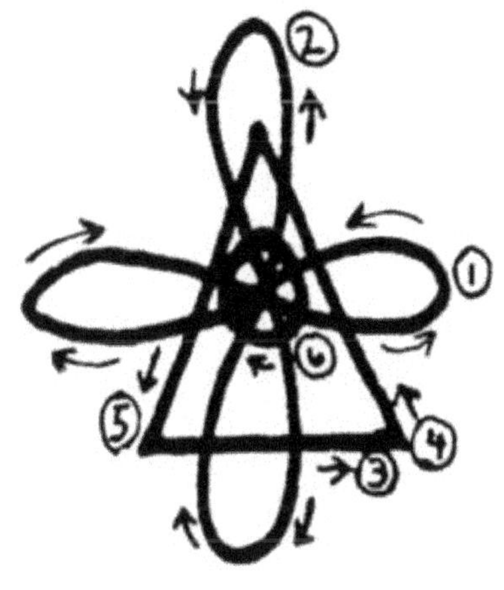

Gnosa is pronounced, "Know Sa" and means the mystical and spiritual knowledge acquired through feeling and connection with universal energies. Gnosa helps release our higher self to communicate more clearly in everyday life. As it increases awareness it uplifts consciousness creating a direct connection with universal energies. It helps the merger of the conscious and subconscious mind to increase that inner connectivity. Gnosa is a primary symbol in Karuna reiki. I incorporate it in Usui Reiki. It is very useful when working with a client who is experiencing some spiritual issues or feelings of disconnection.

Tamasura

pronounced as "Tam-a-sur-a" is excellent in helping a client release fear. It is a symbol of strength and power to overcome fear. It tends to quite one's nerves thus allowing a rational examination of that which is responsible for their fear.

Dai Fu Ku pronounced as "Die-"Foo-Koo" involves a very large change in the emotional output of a client. It should be reserved as the last part of a treatment for acute depression, rejection of self, a general malaise. Dai Fu Ku is for happiness. When using this with a client, say it three times aloud or to yourself. Draw it in the air if you are more comfortable with that. You may give a copy of the symbol to the client to hold while you chant the word. three times. It is also acceptable to give the client a copy with the word *happiness* written on it.

Happiness is not a goal to be sought. It is a byproduct.

Eleanor Roosevelt

Aside

It is always acceptable to use a short questionnaire with your clients. I suggest you use one before beginning a healing session. The purpose is two-fold: first, it give s you some idea about the client's issue and second, it provides a barometer of client expectations. Also, assure the client that you are not making negative judgments about the answers. The information will tell you about the potential energy level of the client as well as help you determine your energy level in your treatment of the client. Alcohol, pot, and pain medication all impact the energy out-put of the client and it may have an impact on the healing processes invoked. Here is a sample questionnaire to use before the healing session begins. You are free to use this, modify it or create one of your own.

CLIENT QUESTIONNAIRE

Name (client)

Legal Address

Phone Numbers:

Reason(s) for today's visit:

Please answer the following questions: Circle your answers.

1. Did you consume any alcohol last night? (Yes/No). How many drinks? (One/More than one).

2. Did you consume sweets before coming to today's session? (Yes/No)

3. Did you consume caffeine before coming to today's session? (Yes/No). If yes, how many cups? (One/ More than one)

4. Are you a regular user of marihuana? (Yes/No) If yes, did you use marihuana before coming to today's session? (Yes/No)

5. Are you using any pain medication? (Yes/No). If Yes, did you take that medication before coming in for today's session? (Yes/No).

6. What do you want to achieve from today's session? Two or three sentences will be sufficient.

Sign:________________________Date_____

The following questionnaire may be modified or ignored. I believe it provides valuable information when it comes to doing a healing. As with the previous questionnaire you are free to change, modify, or create one of your own. The more client information you have, the greater the chance for a successful session.

QUESTIONNAIRE TO DETERMINE CLIENT NEGATIVE ENERGY

As a certified cognitive behavioral therapist be assured these questions are not designed to put you in the role of psychologist. The answers will provide you useful insight into a client who has indicated an issue with negative energy.

1. Do you complain? (Yes/No/ Sometimes/ A lot/. (Circle the one that applies.)

2. Do you often discuss what is wrong in the world more than you do with what is right in the world? Include such things as "terrible weather," "horrible traffic," "stupid government," "lousy economy," and "disastrous environment." (Circle all that apply.)

3. Do you criticize? Friends, Neighbors, Government, Social Group to which you belong, the Internet. (Circle all that apply.)

4. Are you attracted to disaster, murders, scandal ridden lives of celebrities? (Yes/No)

5. Do you blame others when things don't go as you expect them to? (Yes/No).

6. Do you feel you have no control over events in your life? (Yes/No)

7. Do you feel like a victim? (Yes/No)

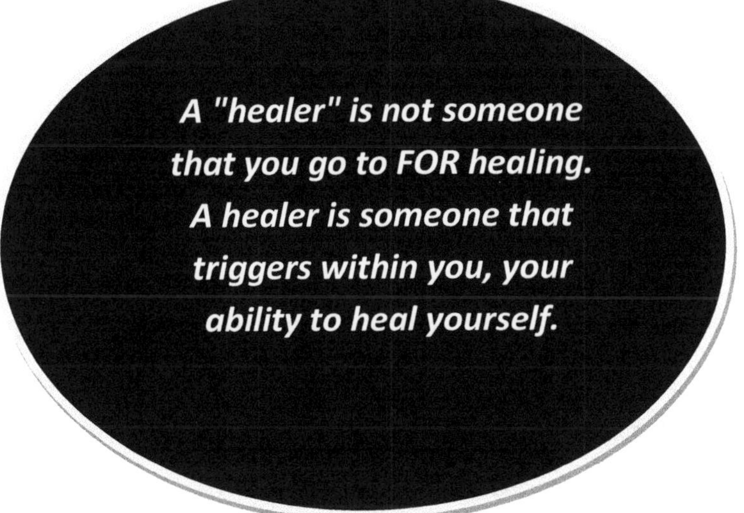

TIME OUT FOR AN ENERGY BOOST

Lest you forget, every healer needs to be aware of her or his energy levels. If you are not up to par, the healing session with your client may not be as effective; therefore to that end, here is a quick and easy way to feel your energy.

ACTIVITY ONE:

1. Fold your hands in the prayer position, over the heart chakra. Vigorously rub them together. Do this for a few minutes, until your hands are warm.

2. Hold your hands about an inch to an inch and a half apart, but still keeping the prayer position. Tune into your hands. You may sense a slight pulsing. You may sense heat bounce from one hand back to the other one. Slowly raise your hands until they are in front of your eyes. Move your hands a comfortable distance from your eyes but,

keeping the hands the same distance apart, and look through the space toward a blank wall. This is your energy field. If it is not bright, you need a boost.

3. Very slowly pull your hands apart and push them back within the inch and half of each other, still in the prayer pose. There will be a very slight resistance. Rub your hands together again. Be vigorous. Repeat the previous steps.

4. Do this as often as needed.

ACTIVITY TWO:

1. Stand up, stretch your arms above your head as far as you comfortably can.

2. Next, bend your left arm over your head and then your right arm.

3. Then gently swing your right arm to the left and back. Do the same with your left

arm. Speed and force are not important; repetition is. Do each of these five times.

HAND POSITIONS TO USE WITH CLIENTS LEVEL TWO

Before working with a client be sure to wash your hands. Spray them with a lavender hydrosol.

When doing distance healing with a doll use the same hand positions that are shown below.

If you are doing a Reiki on an animal use the same hand positions as shown below.

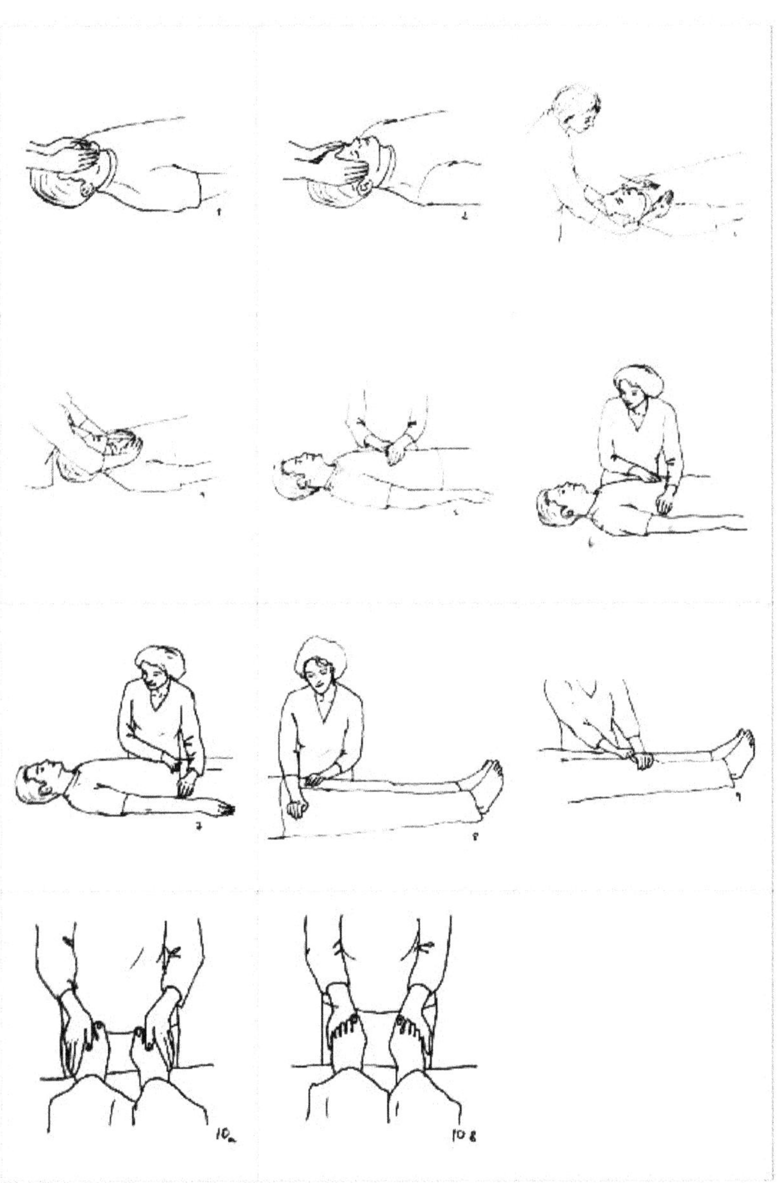

As a rule of thumb, it is a good idea to ask each client permission to physically touch them and to be specific about which body parts are to or not to be touched. Some Reiki Masters advocate the "hover" technique. This involves keeping the hands a couple of inches above the client's body. Notice in the illustration that follows that the Practitioner begins with the head. Elsewhere I have stated I prefer to begin with the feet.

LEVEL TWO ATTUNEMENT

The Attunement for level two involves a stronger emphasis on feeling, sensing, and seeing energy. A longer meditation with an agenda of "letting-go" will begin the attunement. To that end, the following breathing technique will be used. It is an ancient Taoist breathing procedure called ***Ujjayi Breath.*** *(Pronounced as (oo ji e).

Practitioners of yoga may know it as "Ocean Breath"

Ujjayi has the effect of balancing, of releasing irritation and frustration. It helps calm the mind and body; thus, making it more receptive to receiving universal energy. Practicing Ujjayi is an excellent addition to your daily personal heath regimen. It has several benefits. Among these are the following:

1. Increase in oxygen in the blood

2. Builds internal body heat

3. Regulates blood pressure

4. Builds energy

5. Encourages the free flow of your vital life force (prana).

Doing the Ujjayi Breath:

You may choose to be seated, in a seated yoga position, or standing up. I supposed you can do this laying down but I know of no special benefit in doing so.

1. Begin with your mouth closed and breathe in and out through your nose.

2. Make sure the breath you take in through your nose is one that is deeper than your normal breathing pattern.

3. Exhale slowly, emptying your lungs as much as is comfortable.

4. The Ujjayi sound now comes into play. It has been compared to the sound of ocean waves.

Directions for doing this suggest you constrict your throat. For many that has little meaning. I suggest placing your tongue against the back of your upper teeth or your lower teeth and exhale as if you were blowing on a mirror to fog it up. Your mouth should be wide open.

5. I recommend doing this before you begin a healing session with a client. Actually,

do this anytime you to release tension, irritation, and or frustration.

ATTUNEMENT FOR LEVEL TWO

Basically, this is a repeat of the procedures for the Attunement for Level One and those procedures are repeated here. There are few additions.

The Initiation Steps for Attunement Two, Level Two:

The client should be in a seated position, yoga style, on a mat or seated in a chair with both feet flat on the floor and hands held in the prayer position a few inches from the heart chakra. The client's eyes should be closed. I prefer a chair. (It's easier on my back.) I also have some soft music playing in the background. For Level Two I prefer **Solfeggio** frequencies, especially the 528H works nicely.

1. Place your non-dominate hand on the client's head. (Crown Chakra) With your dominate hand draw Hon-Sha Ze Sho Nen, then draw Sei He Ki on the client's left shoulder and finally moving in a clock-wise direction, draw Cho Ku Rei on the client's right shoulder.

2. Come to the front of the client, cup her or his hands, still in prayer position, in yours also in prayer position. Make sure your thumbs lap over the client's hands. Gently move the hands from your Heart Chakra to the client's Heart Chakra. Do this three times.

3. Place the client's left hand her or his right chest. Open her or his right hand and with your index inger draw the Hon Sha Ze Sho Nen symbol on person's palm. Do this three times.

4. Now take the client's right hand and place it on her or his left chest. Open the left hand and draw the symbol for Cho Ku Rei. Do this three times.

5. Lightly tap the pituitary gland three times.[7] This is about where you wear your glasses, at the bridge of the nose.

6. Beginning at the feet, gently "blow' the full length of the body, stopping at the head. Place both hands on the top of the head. The center finger of each hand should be gently touching. Add a slight pressure and hold this position for a full two minutes. If you sense a longer period of time is required for the transfer, use it.

7. Smudge the client with Palo Santo, white sage and copal.

8. Offer herbal tea or lemon infused water.

Basically, this ends the second attunement. Other Reiki Masters may add other items. If they do, it does not diminish the initiation. Each teacher makes the system her or his own, and as they should.

---

[7] The pituitary gland is located in the brain, between the hypothalamus and the pineal gland, just behind the bridge of the nose.

THIRD MANUAL

LEVEL THREE

ATTUNEMENT THREE

THIRD MANUAL

LEVEL THREE

ATTUNEMENT THREE

CHAPETER ONE

INTRODUCTION:

As is usual there is some debate over Level Three. Some view it as distinct from the Reiki Master Degree. Level Three is viewed strictly as a healer practitioner while the Master is viewed as one who is also trained in attuning new student practitioners. Traditionally, the Master is considered one who teaches as well as functions as a healer. Not everyone who trains in Usui Reiki has to teach. There is no prestige added by having the title Master added to one's résumé.

As a personal note, after completing the first three levels, I chose to become a Master so I could teach, since I spent my first career in the teaching field, it felt a natural thing to do. As with all learning, I soon realized there was more, thus my two additional certifications. William Lee Rand in "What is Possible for a Reiki Master?" states, "Because of the nature of the master level and the energies that become available to us, being a Reiki master can be an ongoing process involving continuous personal growth." [8]

At this level, the Reiki attunement may eventually involve an increase in your psychic sensitivity. This may show up as an increased intuitive awareness, an increase in seeing auras and an opening of the third eye.

It's also a good time to remind you that once you have received an attunement, no matter the level, it never leaves you. It is always omnipresent.

There will be five new symbols introduced in this section of which some are designed to enhance your healing menu.

---

[8] The International Center for Reiki Training,

THE SYMBOLS

I may very well be labeled a heretic as I now introduce some aspects of healing from another form of Reiki, Karuna. I will give a gentle nudge that it is still Reiki. The first symbol is called Zonar.

Zonar brings with it a certain mystic aspect and contains certain geometric patterns that hold within themselves meanings. Zonar is composed of the letter Z, and the infinity sign used three times. The purpose or function of Zonar is to heal past lives as well as karmic and inner dimensional issues. To use Zonar, start at the client's head with the letter Z ending at her or his feet.

Draw the infinity sign three times across the client's chest, making sure the heart chakra is covered. I suggest you use this only with patients who have past-lives based emotional issues. Past-lives generally reference other lives; however, I believe it can be past experiences, past memories, for example.

Dai Ko Myo (Pronounced as Dye Ko My O) is probably the most sacred of all the Japanese Reiki symbols. According to some teachers, it is the most powerful of all the symbols; it is the ultimate master symbol. It is revered for its nourishing and enlightening potential. It has the highest vibration and most transformative power of all the symbols promoted by Reiki. In terms of healing, it is all-encompassing. By that I mean it works in the upper chakras, auras, and for many the most important area, the human soul.

Activating Dai Ko Myo:

This high end master symbol enriches healing of every form of Reiki put forth. Generally, it is used with every Reiki healing session whether it is an individual, group, or distance healing. It is a good one to use at the beginning of a healing session. To activate Dai Ko Myo you may draw it on your palm center and then place it on the client's chest or abdomen. You can draw the symbol in the air over the client's body, or saying Dai Ko Myo three times.

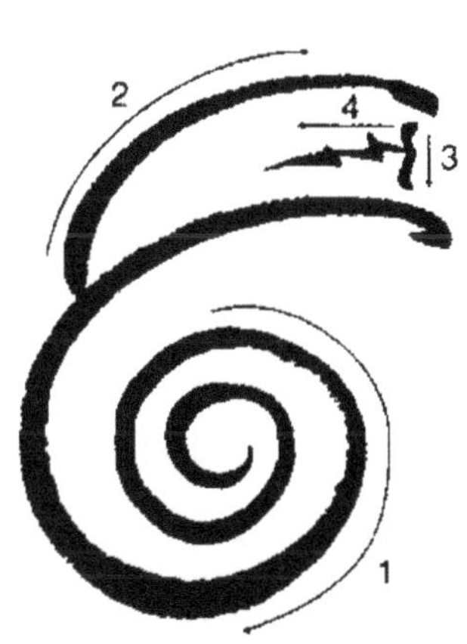

I find it interesting that Tibetan Reiki practitioners use what could be called a twin of Dai Ko Myo. It is Dumo. **Dumo**, (pronounced as *do mow)* is also called Dumo Fire. It is the heat that ascends up from and over the spine. It is said to result in the unification of mind and body produced by the emanation of heat. It is claimed that Dumo pulls negative energy and disease out of the body, our of a room, or situation and releases it. Those Reiki practitioners who use crystals in their practice report that Dumo can be used on crystals so that they self-clean. I generally lean toward Dumo because it's easier to draw. (Actually, I am lazy.)

The next symbol is primarily used by the Reiki Practitioner on those clients who are into the world of the metaphysical. It is also used by the practitioner on her or himself. Unlike the other symbols which are drawn over a client's

body, this one is printed on a card and is to be used as such. The **Third Eye Rising** is designed to activate your Third Eye. Create the symbol on a 4X7 index card, place your dominate hand about two inches above the symbol. Gradually, you will feel the energy flow to your hand. Place your first two fingers on the opposite hand in the center of your forehead, between your eyebrows, about a half inch above them. Keep the fingers in place for at least two minutes so the energy flow can help activate your Third Eye.

Raku (pronounced ray-koo) is considered the final symbol you will receive as you become a Master in the Usui Reiki approach to healing. It is also the final act you will preform as you train clients to become Reiki practitioners. Raku is known as the Fire Serpent. It symbolizes a lightening strike from the heavens that brings the life force. The life force is called *chi.* The function of Raku is grounding the client once the attunement has been passed. To use this with a client, begin to draw the lightening bolt from the top of the head, through the spine to the client's feet. I like to add one other movement here. I place my fingers together (prayer pose without the hands being closed), bring those to my mouth, and blow through them.

ATTUNEMENT FOR LEVEL THREE PROCEDURES

As in the two previous attunements the goal is to prepare you for the acceptance of universal energy, to realize you are a conduit for that energy, and to use it to help your future clients heal themselves.

1. Place your non-dominate hand on the client's head. (Crown Chakra) With your dominate hand draw Hon-Sha Ze Sho Nen, then draw Sei He Ki on the client's left shoulder and finally moving in a clock-wise direction, draw Cho Ku Rei on the client's right shoulder.

2. Come to the front of the client, cup her or his hands, still in prayer position, in yours

also in prayer position. Make sure your thumbs lap over the client's hands. Gently move the hands from your Heart Chakra to the client's Heart Chakra. Do this three times.

3. Place the client's left hand onher or his right chest. Open her or his right hand and with your index finger draw the Hon Sha Ze Sho Nen symbol on person's palm. Do this three times.

4. Now take the client's right hand and place it on her or his left chest. Open the left hand and draw the symbol for Cho Ku Rei. Do this three times.

5. Lightly tap the pituitary gland three times.[9] This is about where you wear your glasses, at the bridge of the nose.

6. Beginning at the feet, gently "blow' the full length of the body, stopping at the head. Place both hands on the top of the head. The center finger of each hand should be gently

[9] The pituitary gland is located in the brain, between the hypothalamus and the pineal gland, just behind the bridge of the nose.

touching. Add a slight pressure and hold this position for a full two minutes. If you sense a longer period of time is required for the transfer, use it.

7. Walk around the student counter clockwise and say Dumo three times. Walk around the student in the opposite direction and say Dumo three times.

8. Smudge the client with Palo Santo, white sage and copal.

9. Play a crystal bowl or a Tibetan bowl for a few seconds.

10. Give the student a few minutes to sit quietly. While the student is resting, prepare an herbal tea or fresh lemon water to offer.

11. Offer herbal tea or lemon infused water.

Debriefing Session after the tea. Presentation of Reiki Master Certificate.

REIKI AND THE USE OF CRYSTALS

A crystal is a homogeneous sold substance that has a natural geometrically regular form with symmetrically arranged plane faces. They are built of atoms whose fundamental building blocks are protons, neutrons, and electrons. The atoms are in constant motion or vibration; thus, creating energy.

The power of crystals lies two specific areas: their ability to amplify energy and second, their ability to hold and transmit that energy. Because crystals have these two abilities they are used in many healing modalities. Since Reiki is an energy based healing modality it makes sense to marry it and crystals for the benefit of your client. There are several crystals that work especially well with Reiki.

Among the crystals that are frequently recommended for use with Reiki are clear quartz, rose quartz, amethyst, agate, amazonite, black tourmaline, carnelian, and peridot. There are many other crystals that you as Practitioner may choose. What do they do for the enhancement of a Reiki treatment? The following chart lists some crystals and what they contribute to the Reiki healing session.

REIKI, CRYSTALS AND THEIR USES

agate	good for protection, enhances longevity
black tourmaline	protects and helps get rid of negativity
amazonite	helps to remove emotional blockages
amethyst	helps to expand consciousness and identifying goals. aids in life after death communications
carnelian	helps to get rid of sorrow
clear quartz	high vibration. good for clarity and understanding
peridot	helps to dissipate angry emotions.
rose quartz	gentle healing energy for emotions

HOW TO USE CRYSTALS DURING A HEALING SESSION

First, always make sure the crystals you use are clean. By clean I mean both physical dirt and emotional dirt. Most crystals can be physically cleaned by just running water over them. Selenite, however, will dissolve in water. Place your crystals in the sun for an hour. If it's not possible, lay your crystals on a bed of sea salt. Never use the crystals on a client before they have been cleaned.

Crystals may be placed around the client while she or he is on the massage table. You may, with client permission, lay crystals on various body parts such as the head, abdomen, or ask the client to hold the crystal(s) in their hands.

Have the power crystals in various places in your healing room.

You may have what is often called a crystal altar. To avoid any religious suggestion I suggest calling it a crystal grid. The primary function of the grid is to magnify the healing energy of a group of crystals, thus promoting the healing of a client. Depending on your taste, a grid can be very simple or complex. Here is a diagram of a grid. You may use this one or create your own.

At each point place a crystal. You can mix the crystals or use one kind at each of the points. You can fancy this up by placing candles between the points. If you use candles I strongly suggest the battery type.

What is an Essential Oil?

"An essential oil is a concentrated hydrophobiic liquid. This liquid contains high aroma compounds and can be made from a wide variety of plants. Because a very distinctive scent or essence, the names used to identify them include the following: volatile oils, ethereal oils, aethorolea oils, and the popular essential oils. There are several ways by which essendces of plant oils are abstracted. Among these are steam distillation, Co2, absolutes, and cold pressing. Steam disillation is the most common method of extraction."[10]

You need to keep in mind that not oils are pure. All too often, oils from other countries have been contaminated. A recent example is the contamination of lavender essential oil

[10] Wilson, Norman W. Healing the Shaman's Way. Camano Island. Mélange Publishing 2017. p. 48.

from France. Know your dealer and ask questions about the place of origin of the oils.

Essential oils have vibrational frequencies just as do the bodies[11] of your clients. As a Reiki practitioner, you are working with vibrations. Remember all things vibrate. This vibration frequency is measured in hertz. See the Hertz Chart on the next page.

[11] The human body resonates between 62 and 72 Hz.

What Is A Hertz?

All plants vibrate; therefore, so do all essential oils. Here is a short list of essential oils and their frequencies.

All atoms in the universe have vibrational motion. Each periodic motion has a "frequency" (the number of oscillations per second), measured in Hertz:
1 Hertz = 1Hz = 1 oscillation per second
1 Kilo Hertz = 1KHz = 1000 oscillations per second
1 Mega Hertz z = 1MHz = 1,000,000 oscillations per second
1 Giga Hertz = 1GHz = 1,000,000,000 oscillations per second
1 Tetra Hertz = 1 THz = 1,000,000,000,000 oscillations per second

Vibrational Frequences of Essential Oils

Rose	320MHz
Helichrysum	181 MHz
Frankincense	147MHz
Lavender	118MHz
Myrrh	105MHz
German Chamomile	105 MHz
Melissa	100MHz
Juniper	98MHz
Sandalwood	96MHz

OTHER TYPES OF REIKI

Tibetan Reiki---Combines techniques from the original Usui Reiki.

Karuna Reiki---Employs sounds transmitted through intention or chanting and is used to heal additions.

Gendai Reiki---Founded by Hiroshi Doi and generally is considered a modern approach.

Rainbow Reiki---Created by Walter Lubeck and employs the seven main chakras of the body.

Five Element Seichem---Founded by Alex Baisley and uses the five elements of the universal life force to promote healing.

Shamballa Reiki---This system uses universal energy, vibratory symbols and healing rays to repair and balance the physical, emotional, and mental reals of the human being.

Kundalini Reiki---Channels energy through the lower base chakra rather than through the crown chakra. Used to help clients overcome trauma and other negative emotions.

Imara Reiki---Focuses on past life and or repressed issues. Used in long distance healing.

BIBLIOGRAPHY

Barnett, Libby, and Chambers, Maggie, with Davidson, Susan. *Reiki Energy Medicine- Bringing Healing Touch into Home, Hospital, and Hospice,* Rochester, Vermont: Healing Arts Press, 1996.

Desy, Phylameana Lila. *The Everything Reiki Book Channel your positive energy to reduce stress, promote healing, and enhance your quality of life,* Avon, MA: Adams Media, 2004.

Ellis, Richard. *Practical Reiki-Focus Your Body's Energy for Deep Relaxation and Inner Peace,* New York: Sterling Publishing Co., Inc., 1999.

Gaia, Laurelle Shanti. *The Book on Karuna Reiki® Advanced Healing Energy for Our Evolving World,* Hansel, CO: Infinite Light Healing Studies Center, Inc. 2002.

Goel, Beena Rani, MDS, and Ashwita Goel. Belgaum, India. Health Care Trust. Healing Through Reiki. 2011.

Haberly, Helen. *Reiki-Hawayo Takata's Story*, Olney, MD. : Archedigm Publications, 1995.

Hall, Mari. *Reiki for the Soul: 10 Doorways to Inner Peace* London, England: Thorsons, 2000.

Honervogt, Tanmaya. *The Power of Reiki-An Ancient Hands-on Healing Technique,* New York: Henry Holt and Company, 1998.

Honey, Chyna. Morrisville, N.C. Lulu Publishing. 2015.

Honervogt, Tanmaya. *Inner Reiki A Practical Guide for Healing and Meditation,* New York: Henry Holt and Company, 2001.

Jewell, Penelope. *Reiki A Guide to Your Practice of Reiki Energy Healing*, New York: Adirondack Press, Inc., 2003.

Lambert, Mary. *An Introduction to Reiki: healing energy for mind, body, and spirit,* New York: Sterling Publishing Company, 2000.

Lotus, Green. "Reiki Really Works A Groundbreaking Scientific Study". Hubpages. com. 2011.

Lubeck, Walter, and Petter, Frank Arjava, & Rand, William Lee. *The Spirit of Reiki*, Twin Lakes, WI: Lotus Press, 2001.

Marques, Joao Antao. A Different Method to Send Reiki. Pantelimon. Romania. Reiki Rays. November 23, 2106.

McKenzie, Eleanor. *Healing Reiki: Reunite Mind, Body and Spirit with Healing Energy,* Berkeley, CA.: Ulysses Press, 1999.

Morris, Joyce J. *Reiki- Hands That Heal,* York Beach, ME: Samuel Weiser, Inc., 1999.

Murray, Steve. *Reiki the Ultimate Guide Learn Sacred Symbols & Attunements plus Reiki Secrets You Should Know,* Las Vegas: Body & Mind Productions, 2003.

Murray, Steve. *Reiki The Ultimate Guide Vol. 2 Learn Reiki Healing with Chakras plus New Reiki Healing Attunements for All Levels,* Las Vegas: Body & Mind Productions, 2005.

Pencyzak, Christopher. Woodbury, Minnesota. Llewellyn Publications. Magick of Reiki. 2017,

Petter, Frank Arjava. *Reiki Fire*, Twin Lakes, WI.: Lotus Light Publications, 1997.

Rand, William Lee. *Reiki The Healing Touch First and Second Degree Manual,* Southfield, MI: Vision Publications, 1991.

Rand, William Lee. *Reiki For A New Millennium,* Southfield, MI.: Vision Publications, 1998.

Rand, William Lee. "What is Possible for a Reiki Master". The International Center for Reiki Training. 2018.

Rowland, Amy Z. *Traditional Reiki For Our Times: Practical Methods for Personal and Planetary Healing* Rochester, Vermont: Healing Arts Press, 1998.

Usui, Dr. Mikao, and Frank Arjava Petter. Shangri-La. Lotus Press. The Original Reiki Handbook of Dr. Mikao Usui.1993.

Webster, Angie. Infinite Reiki, Infinite Healing. Bloomington, Il. Serenity Energy Healing. 2015.

Vennells, David F. *Reiki for Beginners: Mastering Natural Healing Techniques,* St. Paul, Minnesota: Llewellyn Publications, 2000

ABOUT THE AUTHOR

Norman W. Wilson has two doctorates: One in the humanities and one in metaphysical humanism. He is a spiritual counselor and certified as a cognitive behavioral therapist. He is a Reiki Master with two additional certifications in Usui Shiki Ryoho. He holds a certification of completion in Qi Gong for Health and Healing. Dr. Wilson is a trained shaman. He is the author of a dozen books and hundreds of articles on various venues on the Internet. In addition, Dr. Wilson is certificated to use crystals with Reiki and is a certified crystal practitioner.

ALSO BY NORMAN W. WILSON

Textbooks:

Butterflies and All That Jazz with Drs. James G. Massey and Arthur J. Powell

Windows & Images: An Introduction to the Humanities with Drs. James G. Massey and Arthur J. Powell.

The Humanities: Contemporary Images

Nonfiction:

Shamanism What It's All About

DUH: The American Educational Disaster

So You THINK You want to be a Buddhist?

Promethean Necessity & Its Implications for Humanity

The Sayings of Esaugetuh, the Master of Breath

Activating your Spirit Guides

Shamanic Manifesting

The Shaman's Journey Through Poetry with Gavriel Navarro

How to Make Ethical and Moral Decisions: A Guide

How To Get What You Really Want

Fiction:

The Shaman's Quest

The Shaman's Transformation

The Shaman's Revelations

The Shaman's War

The Shaman's Genesis

The Making of A Shaman

NOTES